MOBILE HOME PARK LIVING

A Brief Discussion

Barbara Fox

This is a booklet to give the reader information regarding living in a mobile home park. The examples given are from my experience in the real estate industry. Names have been omitted from the examples for their privacy. Testimonials are from real people. Some have been edited to make the review shorter but not to change the flavor of the review. Their initials are noted.

First Edition 2024

Published with help from 100X Publishing.
www.100xPublishing.com

Print ISBN: **979-8-9909224-0-2**

TABLE OF CONTENTS

PREFACE

Mobile homes/manufactured homes vary in age, size, and condition. For the sake of this booklet, I will refer to them as mobile homes, as this is common language when referring to mobile and manufactured homes. All mobile home parks have rules and regulations that vary from park to park. Some parks enforce the rules more consistently than others. I've found that by driving through the parks, it is easy to see the degree to which the standards are or are not enforced by park management.

Why did I write this? Having been in the real estate industry since 2005, there are common questions clients ask about mobile homes. This booklet is written with the intent of giving you some ideas and thoughts to consider as you think about your next step in home ownership.

INTRODUCTION

Trailer, mobile home, manufactured home? Call them what you like, but this booklet is for people considering a lifestyle change; those who want to know more about living in a mobile home park and the process to make that happen.

This is a brief overview to address many of the questions people may have when considering purchasing a mobile home in a park.

It's important to understand how mobile home parks work. For example, people see the advertised price of the mobile home and think, "Great, I can afford that!" However, when they find out that the home is in a park on leased land, they realize it's a much higher monthly commitment.

Read on for helpful mobile home park living tips.

CHAPTER ONE

A BIT OF HISTORY

Did you know that in California mobile homes quit being made after 1976? The United States Department of Housing and Urban Development adopted standards in 1974 that went into effect in June of 1976, making manufactured homes safer and built with higher standards. At that time, the name was changed from mobile home to manufactured home.

So, what is a manufactured home built after June 15, 1976? It is a house constructed in a controlled factory environment and built to the federal Manufactured Home Construction and Safety Standards (HUD Code).

Prior to 1954, did you know they were called trailers? Yes!

Remember trailer parks? The name was upgraded to *mobile home parks* in 1954.

In case you are interested in learning more about government building codes for mobile/manufactured homes, there is a lot of information available online. Since building codes are periodically updated, I am not covering that topic in this booklet.

Things to Consider:

- What is your earliest memory of a mobile home park?
- Did you know manufactured homes are built according to HUD code?

CHAPTER TWO

PROS

Ready to make a move? Not sure yet about mobile home parks? Is that you? If so, I've written this booklet just for you.

Let's talk about the PROS first—always a more positive place to start!

#1: MORE LIVING SPACE

Mobile and manufactured homes often offer more square footage. For example, in the spring of 2024 in the Central Valley of California, small apartments (1,000 square feet or less) are renting for $1,700 to $2,000 per month. If you own a mobile home in a park, leases are averaging from $800 to $1,000 in the same area and your living space could be from 1,200 to 1,800 square feet, with 2 bedrooms and 2 bathrooms or even 3 bedrooms and 2 bathrooms. These rent and lease estimates don't cover the cost of the home itself.

#2: EASY-CARE YARDS

Most of these leased lots offer a small area for yard, shed(s), and usually parking for up to two cars. You could put in a small lawn and plants if you enjoy gardening. The limited space also allows for hardscaping. Hardscaping can include bricks, pavers, rocks, poured cement, etc.

#3: GATED COMMUNITIES

While not all parks are gated, many are. This can add an extra level of security to homeowners. The gated communities usually have a code or electronic key to gain access.

#4: MANAGEMENT OF THE COMMUNITY

There are rules for living in these communities. On the plus side, if you have a noisy neighbor who wants to party late and play loud music at all hours, that won't be allowed within a park. Usually, the parks have "quiet hours" that start at 10:00 p.m. and last through the night. Of course, park rules vary. Management will also be responsible for you following the rules of the park. Some parks will bend their rules depending on your situation, but it varies by park and can even change over time. If you have a park you want to live in, it's always a good idea to stop by the park office and discuss their rules to see if the park is a good fit for you. Another good idea is to drive around the park (watch the posted speed limit) and observe the condition of the homes, green spaces, community buildings, and amenities. Possibly visit the park at different hours of the day also.

#5: ANIMALS

Parks govern the type and number of animals you can have on your property and whether they can be outdoors. Some will allow one or two dogs. Usually, they will limit the weight of the dog. The most common weight restriction is 25 pounds or less. Also, some parks will allow cats, but it is common for them to require you keep your cat indoors. If you are concerned about the type or size of animal you can have, check the rules of the park.

Some parks have also banned entire breeds. It would be rare to see a large dog allowed in a mobile home park unless it is a well- trained service dog.

#6: LESS EXPENSIVE THAN A SINGLE-FAMILY HOME

The cost of living in California has gotten so high that people have been priced out of the market and are now considering living in a mobile home park.

#7: COMMUNITY

Yes, you do live close to people in a park. Unlike many suburban communities where everyone is siloed in their homes, mobile home communities can be a friendlier place to live. So, if you've been lonely in the suburbs, you may enjoy having more opportunities to socialize.

#8: AGE RESTRICTIONS

I've put this in both the pros and cons area. The plus is you won't have teenagers racing their cars around or playing loud music. Usually, the over 55 parks are quiet because of the lack of children and teenagers.

#9: STAYING NEAR FAMILY

As pricing in the housing market continues to rise, living in a mobile home park may be the only option to stay near family.

#10: LIVING CLOSE TO YOUR NEIGHBORS

This is another one for both the pros and cons lists. I've met a lot of unhappy seniors in the suburbs, as they are very lonely. In a park, even if you don't want to converse with others, you will see other people going about their daily lives. Plus, you aren't far from others if you need help or assistance.

Things to Consider:

Which of these PROS are most important to you?
- ☐ More living space
- ☐ Easy-care yards
- ☐ Gated community
- ☐ Community management
- ☐ Animals
- ☐ Less expensive to buy
- ☐ Community
- ☐ Age restrictions
- ☐ Staying near family
- ☐ Living close to your neighbors

CHAPTER THREE

CONS

#1: THE IMPRESSIONS/OPINIONS OF OTHERS

One of the biggest barriers I've seen when someone is considering changing their lifestyle by moving into a mobile home park are these concerns: "What will people think?" "I never thought I would have to live in a mobile home park?" If this is something that will bother you, it's something to take into consideration.

#2: IT ISN'T REAL PROPERTY

Mobile homes in parks are not considered to be "real property" like a manufactured home on a permanent foundation. This limits the financing available to buyers. Buyers often ask me about new home loan programs for first-time home buyers that can cover some of their expenses. Mobile home park units to not qualify for those types of loans.

#3: PARK LEASES WILL GO UP

Yes, just like rent and taxes, they do increase. The good news for some California residents is, some counties put in rent control for these parks. So, check the rules of the park; many of them designate the rate of increases so you can plan ahead. To learn more about any rent stabilization in the park you're interested in, check out this website:

California Mobile Home Park Space Rent Stabilization Ordinances (RSO, SRSO) **mhphoa.com**.

#4: LIVING SO CLOSE TO YOUR NEIGHBORS

Only you can determine if this is something you are happy or unhappy about. You should expect to hear more noise from nearby neighbors than when living in a single-family home.

#5: AGE RESTRICTIONS

Over-55 parks have special tax breaks and will lose their designation if they allow you to break the rules regarding residents' ages. One person must be 55+, and the second person usually needs to at least be 45 (I've seen some that allow 40 years old). Or some parks will require everyone to be over 55. They do have special considerations for caregivers. But, no, you won't be able to move your grandchildren in or other people below the age limit unless they're a qualified care giver.

#6: VALUES DON'T APPRECIATE LIKE A SINGLE-FAMILY HOME

I've read some very popular financial advisors saying it's always a bad idea to purchase a mobile home due to their value always depreciating. I haven't found that to be the case in California if you maintain the unit. But, yes, in general, mobile homes are cheaper per square footage. Their value will fluctuate with the housing market.

Things to Consider:

Which of these CONS are of biggest concern to you?

☐ Impressions/opinions of others
☐ It isn't real property
☐ Park lease amounts going up in the future
☐ Living close to your neighbors
☐ Age restrictions
☐ Values don't appreciate as well

CHAPTER FOUR

DO I QUALIFY TO LIVE IN THE PARK?

There are basically two types of parks: all-age parks and over-55 parks. If you want to purchase a home in a park, you'll need to get approved by the park management to lease the land the home sits on. The process is very similar to filling out an application with a property management company to lease or rent a home or apartment. You will need to obtain an application, complete it, and supply the completed application and the documents requested for the park management or owner to review. The review can take anywhere from a couple days to two weeks (usually at least ten days to two weeks). There will be an application fee for anyone living in the unit over 18. Everyone over the age of 18 will need to fill out an application. Some parks will require to meet you in person.

Below are some common requirements that are park specific:

- Credit checks — different parks require different credit scores, typically higher than 650. I've seen some as low as 600.
- Background checks
- Income requirement — typically 2.5-3 times the monthly rental fee.
- Pets (usually under 25 lbs)? None? One or two? Dogs? Cats? If service animals don't comply with park rules, proper documentation is required to allow them to live in the park.
- Number of vehicles

All-Age Parks: No age restrictions

Over-55 Parks: The park can lose their tax benefits if they allow violations of their age rules. Some over-55 parks will require all residents to be over 55 years old. Some may limit the number of people that can reside in the unit. Park requirements may allow one other person to live there if they're over 40 or 45 years old. There are special circumstances and exceptions for a younger, live-in caregiver. However, some parks are requiring doctors' orders that show a resident requires a caregiver. This has happened because some people have been claiming a younger person is a caregiver when they are not to get around the park's age rules.

Things to Consider:

- Considering rules that many parks have, would living in a mobile home park be feasible for you?
- Would you pass the credit and background checks?
- What are the ages of those who live with you?

CHAPTER FIVE

DOES IT MAKE FINANCIAL SENSE?

Renting vs owning is a question individuals must answer for themselves. Rents keep climbing in California, and people are exploring how they can own something of their own. A mobile home in a park might be the right decision for you.

Financing a mobile home in a park

Lenders for mobile homes in parks (manufactured mobile home lenders) are different than traditional single-family home lenders. Lenders have higher interest rates for mobile homes in mobile home parks. Typically, the rates are 1.5% to 2% higher than for single-family homes.

Purchasing a mobile home is more like purchasing a car or RV. Like a single- family residence, an escrow company is used to transfer the title to the new owner. Escrow/title companies are third parties to the transaction that insure the title is clear and the transfer is completed correctly.

There are fees for having an escrow company transfer the title, and I believe it is worth it. I wouldn't recommend handling transferring the title on your own unless you are an expert in that field. The fees are much lower than when purchasing a single-family home.

The lender will have rules about your debt-to-income ratio. They will use both the mortgage payment and park lease when calculating your loan qualifications. As with any loan company, they will consider your credit scores, income, debts, etc., when seeing if you qualify for a loan. If you pay cash for the mobile home, you would only be responsible for the monthly park fees. In certain parks, some utilities may be included in your park fees.

Utilities are another aspect of what your monthly costs will be.

The age of the mobile home will also be a factor when considering downpayments, etc. The loan company will also be doing an appraisal to make sure the mobile home is worth what you are buying it for, and you, as the buyer, will be expected to pay for the appraisal.

Cash buyers would be able to complete the transaction quickly and bypass the need for an appraisal.

Below are two companies that offer manu-factured home loans for park units.

First, if you have good credit, I've found Credit Human to do the best job.

Credit Human
www.mhloanapp.credithuman.com
Phone: 877-475-6852

If you need more assistance, this next broker can help; they work with several companies, including Credit Human.

First Pacific Financial Loans
www.Firstpacificloans.com
Phone: 800-460-0019

Next are some examples of people I've helped in their decision to live in a mobile home park.

Example #1:

The buyer paid $74,000 for the mobile home and financed it (interest rates were low at the time). They had about $8,000 dollars in down-payment, loan fees, and closing costs. They now have a larger place, they own in a gated community, and for less than they paid for their rental. It is about $1,400 per month for their loan payment and park lease fee combined.

Example #2:

They chose to sell their large home and purchase a mobile home to decrease their monthly living expenses. The husband was ill and disabled, and their monthly expenses were higher than their monthly income. They chose to pay cash for a double-wide mobile home, and they pay just under $600 per month for the park lease fee. Their monthly income is now enough to cover their expenses, and they are no longer stressed about meeting their monthly bills.

Example #3:

A newly divorced woman was getting enough money in a divorce settlement to pay mostly cash for a mobile home in a park. The seller did a small owner financing for a couple years for the balance. The buyer was able to afford the park lease fee with her monthly income and pay off the small loan the seller gave her.

Example #4:

A senior couple was running out of savings and couldn't afford to keep their single-family home. They were able to pay cash for their mobile home and stay in the same community with their children and grandchildren. Otherwise, they would have needed to move out of state.

Things to Consider:

- Would purchasing in a mobile home park make financial sense for you?
- Which example Barbara shared is most similar to your situation?

CHAPTER SIX

WHAT NOW?

I hope this brief booklet has helped you learn a bit about purchasing and living in a mobile home park. More questions? My contact information is below. I'd love to hear from you.

Barbara Fox, Realtor®

Email: barbara@othersrealty.com
Call or text me at 209-499-3424.

Barbara Fox is a licensed California Realtor®.
License #01514815

Notice:

Providing this booklet is not intended as a contract to represent the recipient or solicitation of business if the party is already represented by a real estate agent.

TESTIMONIALS

Below are some testimonials from my customers who purchased in mobile home parks.

I recommend Barbara Fox to many because she made me feel valued and respected. She is friendly, listened to my needs, gave me options by showing me different properties, and was with me throughout the purchasing process. She is also very reliable, understanding, and much more.
—MJ

Barbara has helped my family with selling and buying properties for several years. We trust her to look out for our best interests. When it was time for us to purchase a mobile home in a park, she recommended another Realtor® that could help us get the best deal (they specialized in the park we were interested in). —DW

What can we say about Barbara Fox? She is absolutely the best Realtor® agent we have ever had, and believe me we've had a few. We met Barbara over 15 years ago when she helped us buy a house in Lathrop, California. Then, she helped to sell our mobile home that we were living in Lathrop. Next, she helped us buy and sell our house in Lathrop, California, and buy a mobile home in Lockeford, California, over six years ago. In my opinion, she is the most helpful person in this business that you will ever meet. She really listens to our needs and what we are able to afford and never tries to discourage us and try to sell us something that was out of our budget like some of the other agents did. I think I drove her crazy at times, lol, because we looked at a lot of stuff, but she was always there and never once made us feel like we were inconveniencing her in any way.
— D & DC

AUTHOR BIO

Barbara Fox has served her real estate customers in the Central Valley of California since 2010. Her current brokerage, Others Realty, was originally started by her son Saul Carter. He named it Others Realty after hearing the story of how the Salvation Army telegraphed "Others" to their soldiers during the Christmas season. It's a constant reminder that we are here to serve others.

Barbara has spent her life on the West Coast — living in Oregon, California, and Baja California. She worked in Fortune 100 companies, working her way up from accounting manager to Multi-plant General Manager. Her experience was in Accounting, Management, and Organizational Change, and received her BS in Administration later in life, attending college at the same time as her son.

After Barbara left her corporate career, she obtained her real estate license and moved to Baja California, Mexico — a fulfillment of her husband's dream of an ocean-view home! In Mexico, Barbara was involved in rotary and sold real estate part-time while there.

When her husband's health declined, they relocated to Modesto, California, where she was able to be a caregiver for her husband and work part-time as a real estate agent.

Widowed in 2016, Barbara continued to work in real estate, earning her way into the Master's Club — a yearly designation that acknowledges excellent sales performance — during four of the last six years. Her background in corporate America — extensive training in environmental, safety, negotiations, property maintenance, business management, contracts, etc. — have given her an ability to look out for her clients' best interests.

Barbara currently attends a local church, is a board member for We Ignite Nations, and is involved with 100X, a Kingdom movement focused on expanding the Kingdom of God. In her spare time, she enjoys gardening (Master Gardener with the University of California), hiking, and spending time with family and friends. She has two rescue dogs, Lily and Crema, and also loves cats!

Other than Sunday evenings when cooking dinner for her family, Barbara is available to help Modesto-area residents with real estate information and buying and selling.

Contact Barbara Fox now at
209-499-3424 (text) or **barbara@othersrealty.com**.

Thank you for reading!

MOBILE HOME PARK LIVING

A Brief Discussion

by Barbara Fox of
Others Realty